Resistance Fantasies

ALSO BY DIANE THIEL

The White Horse: A Colombian Journey (2004)

Writing Your Rhythm:
Using Nature, Culture, Form and Myth (2001)

Echolocations
(Winner of the Nicholas Roerich Poetry Prize, 2000)

Cleft in the Wall (chapbook, 1999)

Resistance Fantasies

POEMS BY

Diane Thiel

STORY LINE PRESS
ASHLAND, OREGON

Published by Story Line Press
Three Oaks Farm
PO Box 1240, Ashland, Oregon 97520-0055
www.storylinepress.com

This publication was made possible thanks in part to the generous
support of our individual contributors.

Cover art: "Apollo and Daphne" (1908)
by John William Waterhouse
Book design by Sharon McCann

Library of Congress Cataloging-in-Publication Data

Thiel, Diane, 1967–
Resistance fantasies / Diane Thiel.
p. cm.
ISBN 1-58654-038-6 (paper)
ISBN 1-58654-039-4 (hardcover)
I. Title.
PS3570.H4418R475 2004
811'.6--dc22

2 0 0 4 0 0 1 1 9 3

Acknowledgments

My thanks to the editors of the following journals, in which these poems appeared:

America: "Resistance Fantasies" (Foley Award Finalist)

American Literary Review: "Baba Yaga"

American Poetry Journal: "Sevenlings for Akhmatova"; "Learning Math"; "Wild Horses, Placitas"

Artful Dodge: "Context"; "Growing Up German in Miami Beach"

The Dark Horse (Scotland): "Editorial Suggestive"; "The Fitting"; "Aerodynamics" (reprint)

Carolina Quarterly: "Three Blues"

Connecticut Review: "Tomb of Persephone (Vergina, Greece)"; "Medea in Colchis"

The Hudson Review: "A Knife"; "Power Outage"

Kalliope: "Continuum"; "Punta Perlas, Nicaragua"

Louisiana Literature: "If You Don't"; "Night Letter"; "Naked"; "Bridges"; "Imperial War Museum"; "Rural Aubade"; "Instinctive"

Midwest Quarterly: "Blue Heron"

Mi Poesias: "Lost in Translation"; "Catacombs (Under Odessa, 1943)"; "Women of Souli"; "The Cottage"; "Fresh Water Furnace"

National Poetry Review: "Pushkin and the Black Sea"; "Nursery Shellgame" (Both poems featured by Verse Daily)

New England Review: "Another Changeling"

Notre Dame Review: "Black Sea Acrostic"; "Iphigeneia (Sapphics from Tauris)"; "Elegaic Labors"

Rattapallax: "Daphne"; "Aerodynamics"

Shuykill Valley Journal: "Daphne"; "Aerodynamics" (reprints)

Smartish Pace: "Lines About Love"

Susquahanna Quarterly: "Letter Never Sent"; "Ursa Major in the Hall"; "Immortal Gossip"; "Housekeeping"; "Killing Time"; "Letter from Constanta"

Tundra: "Night Lyrics"

Several poems from this collection have been selected for reprint in the following anthologies:

Literature: An Introduction to Fiction, Poetry, and Drama, 9th Edition, Addison Wesley Longman: "Two Correspondences"; "Ancestral Burden"

Kindled Terraces: American Poets in Greece, Truman State University Press: "Daphne (A Photograph, 1930)"

Deep Travel: Contemporary American Poets Abroad: "Lost in Translation"

Global Poet Network Anthology: "Night Letter" (translated into Korean)

Rising Phoenix, Word Press: "Daphne (A Photograph, 1930)"; "Editorial Suggestive"

My gratitude to the Fulbright Program which funded my year in Odessa, on the Black Sea, where a number of these poems were conceived.

For Alexander,
in the summer of your birth

Contents

Although this land is not my own,
I will remember its inland sea
and the waters that are so cold

the sand as white
as old bones...

—Anna Akhmatova

I.

Black Seas

Black Sea Acrostic

Perhaps when Catherine took her carriage through
One of them, her voice caught in her throat and she
Trembled without knowing why. After all,
Every house looked peaceful, settled, well on its way,
Mirroring her hopes for the new region—Odessa, Crimea
Kherson—filled with rosy children. She couldn't have
Imagined what these simple machinations would
Name, all over the world, for centuries to come:

Vows, unfortunately, come to mind across the years as equally
Illusory, as do the smiles forced through a crack in the front door, the crystal
Lying red and broken moments before, swept under the couch. Small talk
Leaking silence, silence gagging every small sound. We haunt that house,
Apparitions with blood and bones, heavy with bags, headed elsewhere,
Gathering what we can, wandering old towns, yet somehow always
Ending in that first one, fingers raw at that latched closet door.

Daphne (A Photograph, 1930)

I know, in that moment caught, how she was fleeing—
her face eternally still, her body taut,
training every tendril of her being,
holding her in place—the raised knot

of her face eternally still, her body taught
by years of silence, that straight upper lip
holding her in place—the raised knot
of an old laurel tree, the tightening grip

of years of silence—that straight upper lip
we remember so much from the past. Poised, she stands
like an old laurel tree—the tightening grip
of that long summer falling like earth through her hands.

We remember so much from the past. Posed, she stands
by that field where she fell, her face in the hot grain
of that long summer, falling to Earth with her hands.
She would grind by stone and eat the seeds again

by that field where she fell, her face in the hot grain,
her mouth still. Closed. No one would see the swell
she would grind by stone—and eat the seeds again
that next Sunday at the cool garden table.

Her mouth still closed. No one would see the swell,
training every tendril of her being,
that next Sunday, at the cool garden table.
I know, in that moment caught, how she was fleeing.

Iphigeneia (Sapphics from Tauris) ✓

Song has come tonight to allow my questions.
How did I arrive on this unknown ocean?
Life passed in the fall of that long blade, only
following orders.

Sacrificed for "favorable winds" but somehow
plucked from Charon just when I tasted iron.
Someone took my place. I could feel the bones and
flesh fill the space left.

Blood in my eyes, I could feel fur and skin wrap
round me, hear the voice that was not my own, scream
out—in language all of us understand, yet
let it be uttered.

If we survive, memory makes one part split
from the other. One of me died that evening.
One of me seems safe, but will always carry
Fear like a stone child.

Now, with wine-dark hands, I am made to carry
out the very act which my scars remember.
How can I allow yet another brother
such final terror.

Medea in Colchis

This is where it took place. Here. And here.
In this wave. On this dais. In the nether regions
of this heart, on the shores of this Black Sea.

I've heard tell of a mythological woman
who, when faced with such betrayal,
tucked her children in,

a cup of milk beside each bed,
towels stuffed under their bedroom door
and went to the gas in the kitchen.

Dying—she did it exceptionally well
and martyred so beautifully. What control it takes
to tuck everything in place

before you go to the bottom.
My children lie at the bottom of this ocean,
and I still haunt these Black Sea shores:

Notorious witch—who killed everyone she ever loved,
who was raised on the milk of knowing.
We all know it's true—Hell hath no fury.

In the beginning, I was willing to kill for you.
Nothing changed. Later, I was still that willing.
Once there was murder in my veins,

it made the unthinkable entirely
true. Why should it surprise you to find me
so capable of killing more of my own?

Are we all so capable
of anything—in a moment of passion,
that raging fire we go to again and again?

I wish it would have been otherwise,
that Jason and I would live out our lives
in stillness, grow old together.

I wish I never would have made history,
so many dramas, poems. I would be a footnote
instead of a volume.

You who judge—remember—I am not
a safe little myth like your fictitious lives.
I am the darkness that lives inside

every one of you and reminds
of the fifty-one ways to leave your lover—
how we might all think of the fifty-first

at such a moment of betrayal, and the lifetime
of ways to destroy your children, over
and over again, like a dream that never ends.

And you—dear reader, why are you
drawn to my ghastly story?
Do I remind you how hard it is to create,

how easy to destroy?

Tomb of Persephone
Vergina, Greece

I see her here, that desolate girl who spends
half her days in that body beneath the earth.

She'd go anywhere with anyone,
find herself in a tomb on the other side of the world,

drink herself into a place of no return.
She'd like to say she traveled for adventure,

but really she was looking to erase his hands,
erase his voice, erase that night.

Does tasting fear condemn a part of our lives
to the underworld we help create? I understand

the abduction frozen in time, that one moment
becoming the one that memory chooses to entomb.

Forever now, her friend Kyane crouching beneath her,
numb with fear. Her mouth rubbed out from years

beneath the ground. Her hand raised in defense,
that central wheel turning beyond their control, the image

grown huge – not even all the years entombed
can fade his features, drawn in short sharp strokes,

the wheel's spokes spinning round like blades.

Baba Yaga

Do you come here of your own free will?

The question she put to travelers.
Her name implies wisdom, but every Russian child
learns early on not to trust titles.
A simple question cannot be answered simply.
If you answer no, Baba Yaga will eat you.
If you answer yes, she will eat you.
Sphinx-like, she waits inside her fence of bones
for inevitable travelers, asking only

Do you come here of your own free will?

Her mouth stretching from earth to the gates of Hell.
Her hut is always turning, but its door
is always open to the darkest part of the forest.
How did Vasilisa and Ivan survive?
Vasilisa knew not to ask about the skeleton hands
which appeared from the table to pour the wine.
She swept the house in her quiet way. Ivan knew
no simple line, no *yes* or *no* would earn him his horse—

I come here largely by my own free will
and twice as much by force.

If You Don't
After a line from a Russian song

If you don't have a dog
your neighbor will not poison it

and if you don't have a home
you will not have to run from it

when your father's anger shakes the walls
that don't exist because you don't have a home

to grow up in—nowhere to learn
that the husband you won't have

won't leave you for another woman
won't walk out your door one morning—

because you won't have a door
for anyone to leave or enter through

and you won't have a window
for anyone to see you

and if you don't make plans
they will not need to be changed

like the diapers you won't change
since you won't have a child

who will never change your life
whose tiny fingers you will never hold

because of how hard you never wished
and planned her away so many times

and she won't grow up to hate you
for everything you never did

as if you didn't have a child—and she won't learn
that if you don't have a memory

the past cannot devour you
when you stop moving for a brief

moment. Long enough to let the sorrow
catch the joy you never feel because you

don't want to feel the sorrow
its companion. And if you don't feel—

there will be nothing left to heal.

Catacombs (Under Odessa, 1943)

I.

The midwife stroked the mother's hair—We'll turn
the child, she said aloud, Just breathe.
Inside, she prayed, Turn, turn, child, turn.
Please let her turn. Please let her breathe.
Eyes still filled with the massacre
in the square at the Black Sea harbor,
she tried to calm her charge, assure
this mother of the child inside her
Remembering the children—the piles
sorted out. No—if she could save
this one—she reached and prayed—
There in her palms—she held the child,
her hand in a fierce, tiny fist
declaring her will to exist.

II.

The rest of the resistance (and those who didn't resist)
were gathered in the shallows of the Black Sea
and set on fire. We fled to the catacombs
with what we could carry, came out only at night.
The caves stretched for miles in every direction,
and the Germans hardly knew they existed.
It was the safest place not to be found.

My daughter was born there—underground,
blackened by the soot from our fires.
They held my mouth to save our lives
and muffled the child every time she cried.
Somehow she must have grasped
the circumstances of her birth, or else she learned quickly
what it meant to survive at a time like that.
She spent the first years of her life
hardly allowed a sound.

The Muse

At midnight, as I wait for her to enter
my life hangs by a single thread
Youth, freedom, fame mean nothing
when her apparition flutes beside by bed.

Look, here she comes. She raises her veil
and turns, with an exacting eye.
"Was it you who dictated the Inferno
to Dante?" She answers, "It was I."

(After the Russian of Anna Akhmatova)

Sevenlings for Akhmatova

In the room of the banished poet
Fear and the Muse keep watch by turn.
    —Anna Ahkmatova, "Voronezh," (to Mandelstam)

I.

It comes in threes—the red letter,
the midnight warning in disguise,
the knock that shakes the shutters.

My face learns to have three sides.
One third smiles and waves at the station.
Another slides under and hides.

The last goes to the interrogation.

II.

I might have wanted to be—a painter
a sculptor, a novelist. But there was no money
for canvas. No marble. No drawers.

When they took him away,
they emptied the drawers of his poetry.
But I carried his words always on me,

smuggled volumes out—by memory.

Pushkin and the Black Sea

He came to meet me shortly after
arriving—running down Odessa's Steps,
all ears on that compelling laughter,
all tongues in cheeks on the swing of those hips.
What did he want with all those women?
All he needed was a good swim in
my morning waves, my long caress.
He'd run his fingers—then undress
those inner visions. I'd take him under
where deeper forces loosed and tensed,
his sweet limbs moving with and against
my gentle strokes, my swells and thunder.
Oh—it was always epic with him—
the way he'd meet my Black Sea rhythm.

Elegaic Labors

First, you might have to assemble a motley assortment of figures—
cattle, a three-headed dog, apples, some man-eating mares.

Draw on your childhood survival. Abandoned on some distant mountain.
Raised on the milk of a bear. Ambushed by snakes in your crib.

Harness a fire-breathing bull and then sow that red earth with a dragon's
teeth. Keep an eye on your crop. You may not like what you reap.

Chained to a rock for the sake of that fire—or perhaps you'll be asked to
hold up the sky for a while. Roll that old stone up the hill.

Meanwhile, begin to re-think your approach. Re-direct all the rivers.
Wash out the eons of dung. Clean the old stable of thoughts.

Patiently search for that word that will bound one idea to the next, deer-
like, and will keep it alive. This should take only a year.

Study the pulse of the ocean to learn how to navigate clashing
rocks, how they open and pause—just long enough to slip through.

Gather your crew from the ranks of assorted renditions and centuries.
Travel together a while. Wrinkle the time-line a little.

Then there's the riddle you have to both answer and leave an enigma.
Weigh every tone on the scale. Scale every word to the bone.

Still, you might weave and unweave the same shroud on the loom for a
     lifetime.
Watch the horizon for sails. Wait for the Muse to return.

Or you might spend half your life in the underworld, sorting the words
     like
myriads of kernels of grain. Just to start over again.

Here is the passage. Around every turn of this labyrinth lurks doubt.
Now, in just five measured feet—carefully weave your way out.

II.

Resistance Fantasies

Power Outage

Some might have called it the reckless immortality
of youth, the way I charged through days and wired nights,
ready to take or leave anything with no notice.
Driving drunk through life, even more willing to let
drunks drive me home—drawing stalkers like a siren.

(The night the power went out, I had heard from one by phone.)

Housesitting for an anthropologist, her home filled
with masks, effigies, bones, bound to bring anyone nightmares.
African spears, with patina proving they had been used,
positioned, oddly, in the corner of the bedroom.
A cough in the middle of the night—that noise of things shutting off.

I was suddenly awake. Felt for the phone. Cordless. Dead.

Naked, I leapt out of bed, feeling along the wall for the spears.
The weapon first. Crouching close to the door, my ears
pricked. Every tree brushing the unfamiliar house,
every wooden creak—a footstep. It was that night,
naked in the dark, a spear in my grip—I was ready to live.

A Knife

I always carry, tight on my belt,
a small African knife I've had for years—
the kind that are commonly seen in the North,
which I bought from an old merchant in Algiers.

I remember, as if it were now, the old dealer
who looked like a Goya oil painting,
standing next to long swords and torn
uniforms—in a hoarse voice, saying,

"This knife, here, which you want to buy—
legend surrounds it. Everyone knows
that those who have owned it, one after another
have all, at some time, killed someone close.

Don Basilio used it to kill
Donna Giulia, his unfaithful wife.
And Count Antonio, one night, secretly
murdered his brother with this knife.

Some Italian sailor—a Greek boatswain.
An African, in a jealous rage, his lover.
Hand to hand, it fell into mine.
I've seen many things, but this brings me terror.

Bend down. Look. Here, hold it. It's light.
And see here, the anchor and coat of arms.
But I would advise you to buy something else.
How much? Seven francs. Since you want it, it's yours."

This dagger now tight in my belt—my strangeness
made me take it off that shelf.
Since there's no one I hate enough to kill,
I fear someday I'll turn it on myself.

(After the Greek of Nikos Kavadias)

Women of Souli

Greece, 1803

When the women of Souli
knew the forces were near, they slowly
gathered their things. They could see

the fires in the distance. They dressed
for the invaders in all their finery,
embroidered skirts and crimson vests.

Their men had been slain
and they would all be taken away,
their children given to the troops

to be raised to forget their first years.
The women had practiced for this day,
still burning fires, until the moment when

they knew the final news, gathered their children,
and began to dance with slow steps, turning
faster and faster, toward the cliff ledge

and one by one, they danced over the edge.

Killing Time

Just killing time?
It doesn't translate well.
Killing on my tongue, and I'm
Just—Killing—Time.
In what oil-slick paradigm
can the mongers still tell
us it is just? "Killing Time"—
It never translates well.

Wild Horses, Placitas

This old village is known for its horses, wild herds
which consider these foothills their home. They are said
to have run here for centuries, since they were left
by the conquistadores. You rarely will catch
any glimpse—only traces, the dust cloud kicked up
or the high-pitched calls traveling far in the cold
morning air. Very soon after moving out West,
I encountered them, first those mysterious calls
at the break of a dawn, re-inventing my ear
and my eye and the day and the trail with a still
unexplainable peace, like a long desert rain

but then, suddenly breaking, the radio's news
like a murder.

        Why is it, again and again,
we will know of such beauty just as it is lost,
one herd harvested, auctioned—the lead stallion's neck
snapped, as he tried to resist. On a morning like this,
I can't help but want one, at least one mystery
to remain—I want something that large and that fast
and that—costly—to still be out there running free
to have even the tiniest possibility
on an average morning, on waking, or heading
off to work in the city, our sprawling Albuquerque
to hear their hoofbeats in the valley—echoing.

Rural Aubade

What drove this morning's field mouse, who
having caught her leg in one of the two

traps we nature lovers set the night before
dragged it across the kitchen floor

to catch her head (not quite her neck) in the other—
neither one quite enough to snuff her,

when she saw us, she still scrambled away,
her thumb-sized body and silver-grey

tail twitching, she heaved the two planks along
clamped to her body—her coffin-sized clogs

scraping a trail on the red floor. It wasn't pretty.
Maybe it's time to move back to the city.

Punta Perlas, Nicaragua

Under a canvas set up for the sun,
bound to a stake in the ground, the sea turtle
lay on her back, her fins pierced, a rope threading them.

Rolling her eyes, she watched us pass, her breath
coming in loud gasps, as if not enough
air could ever enter her lungs again.

Left by her side were remains of another—
flesh cut in hand-sized pieces,
filling the bowl of the shell.

How long had she been held? I knew
turtles were kept fresh on their backs like that,
months, even years—on old sea voyages.

Was she captured one night when she came
quietly ashore to dig her nest
and lay her eggs against

the odds of birds and men?

Night Lyrics

Darwinian

Thump thump on the roof
one hungry thing—the other
running for its life

Nursery

Last laugh, last carafe,
spin bottle spin.
Hey diddle diddle,
Feline, Violin.

Ghost Twin

Grew up with a ghost twin
who whispered what had happened:
It will happen again

Imperial War Museum, London

After sitting through the ten minute *Blitz*
in our bunker with twenty other tourists,
we wander back one war to the short maze
of *The Trench Experience.*
Continuous recordings run at each station,
alternating soldiers writing home
with gunfire. We're moved—momentarily
And then quickly moved along by the line we're stalling.
In front of us, the three year old in a toy helmet begins
to fire along with the recordings—
Bang Bang Boom Bang Bang Boom. At the last station,
despite his father's urgent, red-faced coaxing,
he stiffens, stands his ground and starts to scream,
No, I like it here! fiercely refusing to leave.

Bridges

I know my father met them as a child,
angels—passed them under bridges,
huddled together, with their wings folded
under their coats, wrapped around their bodies,
faces like gargoyles, frozen, open-mouthed,
wings blown off and scattered in the ash.

And the small boy with no one left who speaks,
might try to find his father there,
might find himself a man there,
under the bridges, lying face to face
with stone forms that might have been
statues blown from the edges of castles

but weren't.

Continuum

Is it about revenge or forgiveness?
Is there some line we cross when we are finally able to forgive,
when we might look into the perpetrator's heart
and find something other than the darkest spot?

Where is that line—was it one sudden afternoon,
the way the light began to hit the other angle of the room?
The telling of the story brings you closer
every time. It might look like so much anger

filtered through a life—churned, distilled, then stilled
to know the way the rage was crucial in that portion
of the path—first to survive—and then to slowly overcome
the past, to let it free. Though you might always carry

the sadness like a stone, you find the way to wear it differently
and in the telling of the story, you know you're not alone.

Resistance Fantasies

We like to think we would have been
Hans or Sophie Scholl, scattering
anti-Reich leaflets for our lives.

We like to think we would have given
our homes, our future children
for the safety of our neighbors.

We like to think we never could have owned slaves
or better still, that we were abolitionists.
We never would have paid a factory death wage.

We never would have sat at bulging tables
while the potato famine harvested the villages
or packed people into coffin ships.

We hear of every trail of tears:
The only good Indian is a dead Indian
How could the people come to that—solution?

And then we close our newspapers, somewhat
aware of what our investments might support,
disturbed to be reminded, in the news, or in a poem.

We might quietly recognize ourselves
when we hear that all it takes for evil
to triumph is for good people to do nothing

And yet go home to our lives and our Silence,
that true rough beast, hiding in the hole
of our full bellies

so easily convinced there is nothing
we can do. And each of us continues to dream
of having been willing to give anything

at that moment in history, of having been,
at the very least, an active resistor. We were all
the heroes in someone else's war.

III.

Lost in Translation

Context

I understood at an early age
how even the most innocent
words could be transformed
into something grisly
when I added my ethnicity.
In an eerie form of alchemy,
chimney, camp, train
could all lead the mind
to the same reverberating
monstrous refrain.

Playing word association
was not a fun game in my house.
What do you hear in these words,
the counselor asked
and wrote on his yellow pad.
Every object, every word
becoming a train of thought
headed for that dark coven.
Even the old folk way of asking
about my mother's pregnancy—

Little Hans in the cellar?
Or Gretchen in the oven?

Growing up German in Miami Beach ✓

I couldn't hide the fact that I was German.
People knew by my name and by my *Omi*
who sometimes came to pick me up from school.
She only knew a word or two of English.
In third grade, I didn't know exactly what
a Nazi was—but some kind of monster—
In music class, when I recognized
a German song, someone called me one.
The teacher took it to the principal,
and then it was all over school.
We sat that morning in the principal's office,
discussing what a Nazi was, and why
the boy was not allowed to call me one. Still,
I left feeling (though I didn't term it so)
that I was somehow predisposed to be
a monster. It was growing in my throat,
in the language that I'd learned, in the *ch*
sounding harder in the center of every word,
in the way my best friend asked me
never to speak German in her house.

That week we learned some things
about the Holocaust in class.
There was a show on television
about the ship that waited off
Miami Beach in 1939,
its Jewish refugees denied asylum.
The Holocaust had sailed right up to us.
I asked my teachers why the ship was sent
back to the Nazis, when the people knew
that they would die. But no one would explain.

Even the ocean looked different then.
That night, there was one ship heading out to sea.
I walked the coast with my Omi, starting to ask
so many things. She stopped and quieted me.
We had often stood there on that shore,
making up stories of voyages we would take.
But in that moment, the moon's face sliding
from the clouds like a sudden ghost,
I knew what voyages could also be,
what cargo ships might hold—what terrible
leviathan—might anchor off the coasts
of our silence.

Night Letter

It is so still here at night
you can hear each breath rise.
I must have been born with two hearts, maybe more,
because one was lost inside me long ago,
and I am still alive.
There is only a small feeling of loss,
a hole about the size of a tooth.

There was a time I could work my whole hand through.

Our mother once said we have nests inside us,
and we thought it sounded sad, then. Now we just know—
there are some things you never get over, never get through,
that take a different form for every one you do.
Nights, here, I lie awake and remember
two sisters talking about their mother,
as if they knew something she didn't.

Housekeeping

On Friday nights, I'd make up seven beds
and sort the clothes in twenty separate piles.
And then the laundromat at Six A.M.
to get all the machines—we had a system.

My little brothers had the job to guard
the dryers. They'd be marching up and down
with hangers, a persuasive troop of soldiers
announcing every load like a command.

The oldest girl, the folding fell to me,
once my arms could stretch out long enough
to fold the giant sheets my mom had sewn
to fit the two full beds they pushed as one.

And Sundays was the day to sweep and mop.
My dad said it was good to learn to keep
a house, that it was an apprenticeship—
a draft I always knew I had to flee.

For years I was ferocious—not to be
a house-wife-poet—was the way I put it.
On hearing this, a poet friend advised
"just keep a dirty house. And that might do it."

I think back to the word my father used
and wonder now, sometimes, if he was right.
When I apprenticed in that ordered home,
every giant sheet became a poem.

Nursery Shellgame

Maps and mazes are my weaknesses.
So many blue prints in the sand
over-lapping—I leave

a trail of crumbs behind me
that are sometimes gobbled up by morning,
sometimes washed away, sometimes stolen.

It is hard to find the way back
without the lodestone, the lodestar—
how you wonder what you are.

A handful of blue marbles might do
if we were twelve.
But we are so much more than twelve

and so much less—
our lives so full
of so much emptiness.

So many years spent
following the tracks of other things
that would chew off limbs

to free themselves, knowing
they would never grow back—
not like those many pointed star fish

arrowed in every direction
or the winter crab—trading one shell
for another, out of necessity.

Necessity sent me out to sea
somewhat suddenly—she said to me
Make sure you take a ship with you.

Make sure you do.
Even a swimmer as strong as you
needs a ship sometimes—even you.

The Fitting

She knows the armholes
need to be cut perfectly round
so that they heal right.

She says it with pins in her mouth
turns me around and around
measures me

finds me small
but knows there are ways to hide
that sort of thing.

She slips with a pin
runs the needle in her thumb
again, laughs hard.

It was a callus, and every thumb
will grow one over neatly like a scab
after just so many pricks:

all those tiny holes
and half of them on purpose
and half of them perfected into ink

and half of them discolored like a bruise,
the shade of blue determined by how deep
the needle dips below the skin.

Silver hummingbird machine
that mannequin is safe
and hollow now without her arms,

modeling a dress that has no sleeves
because she still believes in
biological rules like some religion

or some chemical escape
that lets her think she still wears arms—
arms complete her shape,

matching silk scarves strapped
to a bedpost
and a waist.

The Cottage

In years when summer left that
bone-white ring around my ankle stretched
taut between one shiver and the next
and everywhere was blue and darker blue
and purpled at the sash around my waist.

In summer years of all those perfect white
long-forgotten dunes that stood beside
each other bearing witness to the light
of storms that brought the elbows
quickly to their knees.

When years made summer turn round like a spit
between the ears and every glance
was like a slow-remembered answer
split across the lip
spreading like an egg dropped in a skillet.

A yellow eye that hardened quick
spit fierce in all that heat
and Mama screaming cottage walls
are thin, far too thin
and neighbors shouldn't know that we are here.
It feels a little cooler now that Dad is gone
The eggs are done and quiet in the pan.

Lightning Rod

Why is it after all these years,
a rain like this still brings
a breathless gasp, even in
these first streaks that flash
the memory of those afternoons,
racing against another storm
already soaked to the skin,
biking home over three bridges
keenly aware as I crossed each one
of my body as the tallest thing around.
That third bridge always the hardest—
pushing pushing the pedals
to outrun the lightning,
pushing the envelope to get home—
my mind filling with the charged memory
of my brother teasing,
Stick out your tongue, and touching
a battery or a live wire to my trusting offering.
How I let that happen more than once
is still beyond me.
In some things, I was quick to learn.
But not trust. I wanted so much
to trust. But I never could
grasp the suddenness of storms.
The next one always caught me out.
And then I'd have to ride it through.
Crouching low, my chin to the handlebars,
as if those inches would mean the difference.
I wondered if my mother knew

her daughter had grown into a lightning rod.
Nothing could get me used to those
Florida storms—the sky darkening
abruptly like a shutter closing,
or like a bruise, to be more honest
about the past
and that sharp electric burn,
the thunder following so fast
so close to home,
but still I'd race it anyway.
I'd never learn.

Fresh Water Furnace

Right now I am one room from the center
of the house, with something like the smell
of gas in the middle of the night,
and someone thinks to light a candle.

There are things better left pure energy.

I sit cross-legged in the center of this room,
pry open live shells, string fresh water pearls,
save the misshapen ones for myself,
the ones that haven't had enough

time to grow over into themselves.

As I string them, I look at each one,
each small shellfish in its shell,
that had to hold this stone
inside itself for life.

Learning Math

The day my neighbor shot himself,
(twice in the head, the whispers said)
we were learning to add two plus two
and not to listen to the news
too close to home.
Three plus three, we drilled
Four plus four, the teacher,
and later my mother, lowered her voice.

I know for sure that at that time
I hadn't yet learned to subtract,
but adding and subtracting
are lessons that will come together
most of our lives.

As the years and losses multiplied
beyond what I could count,
it was the dividing that came easiest for me.
After every evening's lights went out,
and I lay in bed, waiting for the sound of steps
arriving in the night to swallow me again,
I would divide and divide and divide
To divide was to survive.
I remember how I thought
it almost rhymed.

To My Brother Miguel
In memoriam

Brother, today I am on the bench by the house
where you leave a bottomless loss.
I remember how we would play
at this time of the day and how Mama
would lovingly chide us, "Now children."

Now I hide
as before, from all these evening
prayers and hope you will not find me
in the living room, the entryway, the corridors.
Later you hide, and I can't find you.
I remember how we made each other cry
brother—in that game.

Miguel, you disappeared
one night in August, nearly at dawn
but instead of laughing as you hid yourself,
you were anguished
And your twin heart of these extinguished
afternoons is weary of not finding you. Already
shadow falls on the spirit.

Listen, brother, don't be too late
showing up. Or Mama will worry.

(After the Spanish of César Vallejo)

Ancestral Burden

You told me my father never cried
You told me my grandfather never cried.
The men of my lineage never cried
They were steel inside.

As you were saying this, you dropped a tear
that fell into my mouth—such poison
I have never drunk from any other cup
than this small one.

Weak woman, poor woman who understands
the ache of centuries I knew as I swallowed.
Oh, my spirit cannot carry
all of its load.

(After the Spanish of Alfonsina Storni)

Another Changeling

I wish I knew the moment when the switch
took place. I've coursed the rivers of memory
dividing all the routes, the points at which

the tremors started. I labored at the cross-stitch
of my father's life, studied the history.
I wish I knew the moment when that switch

took place in him. Was it when he knew too much
to trust in anything? Did his own childhood story
divide the tangled roots, the points at which

the child was lost—in that black forest ditch.
Another walked on, through the sudden cemetery.
I wish I knew the moment when the switch

found me—so early. But memory is such
an unforgiving path—Charon's ferry
devises tangled routes, the points at which

we try to find our way back through the stretch
of wood, that red thicket of blackberry
dividing all the roots—which point is which?
I wish I knew the moment of that switch.

Lost in Translation

My childhood was filled with untranslatable points
of view—the way the child came under the wheels.
Das Kind kam unter die Räder.

When the child was run over,
it was her fault. Did it have something to do
with the order of things? Children

are disorder—they run under wheels
like lizards. Even the signs on the trains
as we traveled through my father's country

reminded us how much was
expressly *verboten*,
how much our tongues divide us.

What was not my mother's cup of tea
was not my father's beer.
Das ist nicht mein Bier, he'd always say.

Traveling into each new lexicon
is to inhabit a new country,
map its pathways into the mind

Every language a labyrinth, weaving
more than words, but a cultural Psyche,
sorting the grains in the syntax.

In Russia, they lock the doors
not to let thieves in,
while America keeps thieves out.

In Colombia I learned that fear
doesn't ride on a burro—*El miedo
no anda en burro.* Fear hath wings

and the reason given for so many things
is *por sus pistolas*—for your pistols
(just because).

Pushing through a thick net of language
all my life, trying to find some way out
from under the wheels

Always on the shore of another culture
even in this ancient bond—marriage
searching for the words I'd need

to make my way in that new country,
only to be told that there simply is
no word in Greek for privacy.

Only secrecy. Or loneliness.

IV.

Editorial Suggestives

Two Correspondences

The Secret

This page, discreetly, will convey
how, the moment that I read it,
I tore apart your secret
not to let it be torn away
from me—and I will further say
what firm insurance followed:
those paper fragments, I also swallowed.
This secret, so dearly read—
I wouldn't want one shred
out of my chest, to be hollowed.

Chestnuts

Lysi, I give to your divine hand
these chestnuts in their thorny guise
because where velvet roses rise,
thorns also grow unchecked, unplanned.
If you're inclined toward their barbed brand
and with this choice, betray your taste,
forgive the ill-bred lack of taste
of one who sends you such a missive—
Forgive me, only this husk can give
the chestnut, in its thorns embraced.

(After the Spanish of Sor Juana)

Letter from Constanta
For Ovid in Exile

Did you hold this smooth stone,
once rough in your palm?

Did you walk this Black Sea shore
also stripped of your tongue?

How did each new syllable feel
when it took form?

Did you think of Daphne, transformed
or Orpheus, forever wandering in longing?

Did the crack in the universe open here
and pour in light from an ancient song?

Is this where you learned to leave
your language—and live the poem?

Naked

Song, let them take it,
For there's more enterprise
In walking naked.
    —W.B. Yeats

This one always felt
addressed to a certain
thief in your life.
I can hear your voice,
as I sit trapped in this
meeting of packrats,
their little red eyes,
not glittering.
I wish I were off,
naked with you,
William B—
in some enterprise
greater than these
small words,
which, nonetheless,
you whisper—you learned
are sometimes needed
to get on to the next.

Ursa Major in the Hall

Can't bear it anymore—this small hall talk.
I need real talk, long talk, hard talk, hot talk,
slow talk, low talk, talk that slips in my ear
and slides all the way down my backbone,
talk that rides me away without words.
Can't waste it anymore—these sounds I hear
inside my ear—ever more hard to ignore.
Let me warn the gossipers they must beware,
lest I suddenly forget this is a hall
and feel the fur rise on my neck
and smell the chilling wind of Fall,
rise on two legs—growl—and bat them down the hall.
Then growl again and show my teeth
and finish with this copy machine.

Instinctive

Across the miles, I rode the wild
in your voice—wanting something to hold
that spinning night together.

Wait, you said, *the cat
has caught a mouse*
and lay the receiver down.

I thought I liked that moment
for the saving of the mouse,
but underneath, I also wondered how

the story might have otherwise played out.

Letter Never Sent

An empty envelope arrived instead
of your letter—I never heard from you again.
I wondered what the letter might have said.

I should tell you for years I wished you dead,
then mourned you in the notes I never sent.
Your empty envelope arrived instead.

I've long since moved and sold the bed
you cheated with that other woman in.
I wonder if she'd wonder what it said.

I even thought you'd planned it all ahead—
that you would play your usual game, and when
the empty envelope arrived instead

of a letter—No—I'd rather be dead
than ever try to contact you again
or wonder what your letter might have said.

Forget it—in this letter I won't send
I won't wonder, ask or tell you when
that open envelope arrived instead
of what your empty letter might have said.

Retreat

I watch him leave me, see it in the way
his eyes turn to her. It's not a passing thing.
I've known all week. This silent retreat
seems an odd place to lose your love.
I watch him move further and further away.

Heading home, I stay quiet. We drive
for an hour in a storm he doesn't notice.
I think of how to bring it up. My silence beats
fast and loud, a foreign thing inside my body.

We stop for gas. At times like these, the car still needs gas.
I go inside to find the restroom, stand in line,
then leave through the electric eye.
No sign of the car.
Wrong door?
There is only one.
My eyes run the row of pumps.
He's left me
at this convenience store.
He's left me.
I never thought it could happen like this,
at a convenience store
in the middle of the desert.

A tap on my shoulder. He's here, beside me, answering,
"The car? I parked it around the corner, out of traffic. What did you think?"
"I thought you'd left me."

"Left you? How could you think I'd leave you?"
A motorcycle roars up beside us.
"Haven't you?"

Lines About Love

What times are these
When it's almost a crime
To write about trees
                —after Bertolt Brecht

Lines for Love

If you write about love,
some will want to know,
where did your politics go?
Yet in love, we want to save
what, without, we may only
want to leave.

Aphrodite and Ares

The children of Love and War
Aphrodite and Ares
were Phobos and Deimos
Panic and Fear.

The trouble

We know all too well what the trouble is.
We want the very thing that we can't give.

Blue Heron

There was current this morning and debris
from a windy night that blew through the trees,
and the sea grape leaves falling like gifts
he might have gathered from the surface
of the water and given to her in a handful.

As if currents could be caught in a hand
and offered. As if the only thing that mattered
was what passed between their hands.
As if either of them still had some faith
to offer the other. As if they knew

the blue heron that spread its wings
just that moment to take off—was just that.

Three Blues

"Dime con quien andas, y te diré quien eres."
    —Mexican saying

"Tell me who you walk with, and I'll tell you who you are."

Tell Me

And what if
for all your life
you walk alone

telling nothing
of who you are
and claiming

no one

Departure

Tomorrow I will still be
in the wake of your hands
holding my body like you believe

less in word than want and bone
the hour that you turn
your face from mine

and send me on

Old Love Tune

I'd love to lengthen even your name
into sweet syllables I can roll over my tongue—
honey when you're away

Let me sing you an old blues song
Let me call you by the name
of all the wild things

that call you home

Immortal Gossip √

Danae: I should have known. You too?
           What line, what mask did he use with you?

Leda: With me, he came in like a swan,
           but I laid some bad eggs with that one.

Leto: I found myself with a snake
           on my tail, his jealous wife's work.

Antiope: He was a horny goat to be sure.
           But I've always had a weakness for satyrs.

Leda: Poor Semele. She wasn't so lucky.
           Literally burned up by his intensity.

Callisto: And Io, you know, forever the wanderer.
           He turned her into such a heifer.

Leto: All of Europa turned bovine—it seemed
           when he came on like a bull in the Aegean.

Callisto: Yeah, after I got caught up with that prince,
           I've been a bear to all men ever since.

Danae: With me, would you believe it was the rain?
           Held my face to the sky to take it in.

Leda: Well, what can you do—beware
           of every swan, or bull, or sudden mist?

Danae: When he comes to you in a shower
of much-needed rain, how can you resist?

Aerodynamics

For years I tucked them in
the places they might not
be seen—the silvery rhymes
you'd only find when you
tried the poem in the air,
to see if it would fly.

Secretly committing
rhymes—the rhythm rising
from the hips, like heat
into the air—my secret
life unbridled there,
upon your secret lips.

Editorial Suggestive
From a 21st century editor

"What lips these lips have kissed and where and why"—
A hot beginning! What the readers want!
But could the lips be *hips*—get more "up front"
to better wake and shock the weary eye?
Must it be ghosts that tap the glass and sigh?
Why not a well-remembered lad at the front
door? (Or, better at the back?) You won't
quite let him in, but then—No, what have *I*
to say about it? It's your poem, n'est-ce
pas? *Lain*—Good verb—although the lay could be
more tempting. Set the reader's cheeks aflame.
Bend those boughs. Take him up against that tree—
out in that rain! And one more thing—oh, yes—
dear Edna, you must also change your name.

About the Author

Diane Thiel is the author of *Echolocations* (Nicholas Roerich Poetry Prize, Story Line Press, 2000), *Writing Your Rhythm* (2001), and *The White Horse: A Colombian Journey* (creative nonfiction, Etruscan Press, 2004). Her work appears in *Poetry*, *The Hudson Review*, and *Best American Poetry 1999* and is re-printed in over twenty major anthologies from Longman, Bedford, Harper Collins, Beacon, Henry Holt and McGraw Hill, including *Twentieth Century American Poetry*. Thiel received her BA and MFA from Brown University. Her work has received numerous awards, including the Robert Frost Award and the Robinson Jeffers Award. Thiel was a Fulbright Scholar for 2001-2002, in Odessa on the Black Sea, and is on the creative writing faculty at the University of New Mexico.

www.dianethiel.net